The Truth About Silver (Or, As Close as You Can Get to It)

By

Will MacPheat©

Part 1 – The Numbers

First, the Disclaimer

This is not intended to be investment advice. I am simply trying to present the facts as best as I have been able to determine them, based upon research of available information and my personal analysis of what the various numbers mean.

Who I Am

In my lifetime, I have been a geologist, engineer and accountant. I am very good at crunching numbers and at analyzing them to extract meaningful information.

Like you, I am an American citizen who is concerned about the current economy and wondering how to protect my personal assets. To that end, I am evaluating silver and gold as investments.

True or False?

I have bought silver in the past, currently own it, and would like (I think) to have more of it. However, I am skeptical about the various reports floating around the internet regarding silver:

China is buying it!

JP Morgan Chase is short 3.3 Billion ounces!

There are only a billion ounces in above-ground supplies!

Like you, I don't take statements like these at face value. Instead, I research the allegations to find my own answers.

Why it is Hard to Discover the Truth about Silver

For many reasons, finding the actual numbers on silver supply and demand is *very* difficult. Thus, any analysis of silver supply and demand will have gaps.   But I think I can present enough data here to draw some conclusions.

I relied largely on United States Geological Survey (USGS) data. For those that don't know USGS, they are pretty good at what they do and because their info is used by the government for more than one thing, they *have* to be unbiased.

Silver is a Commodity

Like all commodities, price can be determined by speculation as much as by supply and demand. This paper is *not* for those of you who are out to beat JP Morgan Chase at their own game, if it exists. You don't have enough money. If you think you can figure out the trading patterns and ride the artificially contrived ups and downs of any major players in the silver market, then please feel free to do so. You can even send me the info you use to figure it out. I would love to take a look at it.

One Fact is Certain

Precious metals are good to own, at least to some extent, because they provide some protection from economic calamities. And, if you are not rich, silver is the best choice. Seriously, how much gold can you go out and buy with your current cash? Now, how much silver can you buy? Add to that the fact that, from a long-term perspective, silver appears to be seriously undervalued compared to gold.

The Effect of Market Demand on Price

The author of a very good historical analysis of gold and silver production since 3000 BC has concluded that, because the ratio of silver to gold production has historically been about ten to one, the price of silver should be ten percent of the price of gold.

What is wrong with this rationale? It ignores the issue of demand. If there were no demand for gold but a demand for silver, gold would cost less than silver, regardless of how scarce gold was! If the demand for gold were, let's say, ten times the demand for silver, it isn't hard to figure that the price of gold could be 100 times the price of silver.

I meant to save this for the "Picking Apart the Pundits" section later, but I couldn't stop myself from getting on the soapbox. So, I am going to lay out the facts as completely as I have been able to discern them.

After each set of figures, I am going to give my analysis of what the numbers mean. I would like to think that this is the important part, but you will you now have the numbers and can come to your own conclusions:

World Silver Supply, 1493 to 1930

Year(s)	Mine Production
1493-1880	6,207,580,994
1881-1890	1,004,576,877
1891-1900	1,616,373,178
1901-1910	1,826,234,623
1911-1920	1,935,607,379
1921-1930	2,387,189,080
Totals	14,977,562,131

The above numbers show the world's estimated silver production (in ounces) from about the time that Columbus discovered America until 1930. The total is almost 15 billion ounces of silver.

How much was mined before 1493, we don't know (although I'll give an estimate in Part 2, below). Despite being quoted to the ounce, the figures above cannot be entirely accurate. Still, they represent a solid, educated estimate and, as such, are a good guide.

Now, prior to 1930 there wasn't a huge industrial usage of silver. Electronics were just getting started. There was some photographic usage of silver, but that was really a small amount compared to this total.

So where did this silver go? Mostly coins, jewelry and government treasuries. I can't believe that much of it was lost because, historically, people have not thrown silver away and the usual ways in which silver is lost to the world today, the disposal of electronic devices, did not exist.

Sure, some silver would have been lost in shipwrecks, buried with people, or just simply lost. However, the total amount truly lost cannot have been substantial and should have been more than offset by the amount of silver mined prior to 1492. This would suggest that, as of 1930, there were close to 15 billion ounces of silver in world coins, treasuries, jewelry and silverware. I'm not going to discuss the years 1931 through 1933 because they are not significant in the big picture.

The next problem that I encounter in analyzing the quantity of silver is that there is a gap in records from 1934 to 1950. We know that the US melted at least 200 million ounces of silver in the form of coins during the period just after World War I. However, the world also minted a lot of silver coins during the 1934 - 1950 period, and a lot of those are still around.

Figures during this timeframe are also somewhat inaccurate because there was no reporting from communist countries during this era (as well as for some years prior to and after this era). The information at the end of this section, as well as in Part 2, will explain some of the gaps in this data. Suffice it to say that, at the end of this period, there was still a worldwide supply of silver in above-ground stockpiles that included coins, silver bars, silverware, and jewelry.

Although there is a gap in statistics, I am not saying this data does not exist. USGS Minerals yearbooks contain this information at: http://minerals.usgs.gov/minerals/pubs/commodity/silver/. However, to extract the information, you have to go through about 400 pages for each year to get information that is, to some degree, estimated. However the quantities in the USGS records may be – and probably are – excellent estimates.

In fact, estimates are unavoidable in the world of evaluating silver. Fortunately, the actual quantities are not required to determine the historic availability of silver because accurate estimates are available to help us see the big picture.

So, on to another chart:

Silver Supply and Demand 1950 – 1989

Year	Supply				Demand		
	Mine	**Secondary**	**Othe**	**Total**	**Industrial**	**Coinage**	**Total**
1950	169.5	-	-	169.5	157.4	44.1	201.5
1951	165.5		-	165.5	164.6	90.5	255.1
1952	180.6		-	180.6	142.1	114.3	256.4
1953	184.7	-	-	184.7	168.3	90.8	259.1
1954	178.6	-		178.6	160.8	83.4	244.2
1955	187.7	-	10.3	198.0	192.8	52.6	245.4
1956	189.8	30.5	3.7	224.0	215.9	56.6	272.5
1957	195.6	25.0	3.8	224.4	212.6	84.2	296.8
1958	202.3	17.0	1.3	220.6	190.5	79.5	270.0
1959	195.6	33.4	42.0	271.0	212.9	86.4	299.3
1960	201.8	52.0	90.0	343.8	235.3	103.9	339.2
1961	203.9	65.0	181.0	449.9	267.7	136.0	403.7
1962	210.8	69.0	107.0	386.8	273.6	127.6	401.2

1963	214.0	68.0	147.0	429.0	277.1	166.4	443.5
1964	211.5	86.0	374.0	671.5	315.9	267.1	583.0
1965	218.4	103.0	426.0	747.4	355.8	'385.1	740.9
1966	225.2	105.0	217.0	547.2	414.9	129.5	544.4
1967	214.7	126.0	252.0	592.7	399.0	105.3	504.3
1968	230.2	227.0	232.0	689.2	371.0	89.3	460.3
1969	248.7	174.0	119.0	541.7	383.8	32.7	416.5
1970	258.5	127.0	91.0	476.5	372.9	23.4	396.3
1971	247.3	127.0	9.0	383.3	386.6	27.8	414.4
1972	248.9	112.0	14.0	374.9	427.4	38.1	465.5
1973	254.0	122.0	47.0	423.0	516.5	28.5	545.0
1974	236.6	192.0	22.0	450.6	466.3	31.6	497.9
1975	239.0	177.0	21.0	437.0	404.5	33.4	437.9
1976	242.9	235.0	19.0	496.9	481.0	30.0	511.0
1977	263.3	169.0	13.0	445.3	456.8	34.5	491.3
1978	266.8	152.0	16.0	434.8	449.1	39.5	488.6
1979	272.0	216.0	17.0	505.0	445.1	31.0	476.1
1980	264.6	302.0	18.0	584.6	362.5	15.0	377.5
1981	287.5	184.0	12.0	483.5	353.6	9.5	363.1
1982	297.0	155.0	3.0	455.0	359.3	12.0	371.3

1983	313.6	197.5	20.0	531.1	355.2	10.2	365.4
1984	327.8	165.6	--12.0	481.4	372.7	13.7	386.4
1985	336.0	140.9	12.0	488.9	372.5	13.4	385.9
1986	322.3	129.3	-4.4	447.2	406.4	26.8	433.2
1987	340.5	137.9	26.1	504.5	428.1	30.4	458.5
1988	346.4	143.9	14.2	504.5	450.6	25.3	475.9
1989	361.1	136.2	17.0	514.3	469.2	26.3	495.5
Total	9755.2	4502.2	2581	16838.4	13448.3	2440.6	16274.0

The numbers on the last row above are the totals, in millions of ounces. The supply side is broken down into Mine Output, Secondary, and Other. Other would include the melting of scrap, coins, bars, jewelry, and silverware.

The important thing to note about this chart is that the demand categories are only for industry and coinage, so some of the industrial number must include silver for jewelry, silverware, and photography.

Here is my point: During this period, 2.4 billion ounces of silver went into coins. We don't know how much went into jewelry and silverware. There is also a discrepancy of about 350 million ounces between supply and demand, with supply exceeding demand by that much.

If we assume that the "Other" supply category is all from the melting of coins and that none of the demand for that silver was used for silverware, jewelry and silver bars, there would still appear to have been an above-ground increase of at least 250 million ounces of silver during this period.

You could guesstimate how much industrial silver (e.g., silver used in electronics) was reclaimed, but it really doesn't matter. The main point is that above-ground stocks increased.

Note: The world silver supply during this period was about 16.8 Billion ounces, about the same amount that was produced from 1493 to 1930.

Whether the silver was in coins, jewelry, silverware, or silver bars, those silver sources still exist. The silver in them has not been destroyed.

This brings us to our next chart …

World Silver - Supply and Demand 1990 – 1999

World Silver Supply and Demand											
	1990	1991	1992	1993	1994	1995	1996	1997	1998	1999	
Supply											
Mine Production	524.5	512.8	487.6	470.1	452.0	479.7	487.8	526.6	547.8	546.8	
Net Official Sector Sales	-		-	6.0	17.6	25.3	18.9	-	40.0	87.0	
Old Silver Scrap	135.1	141.9	148.3	148.5	151.9	162.9	158.4	169.3	193.7	174.9	1584.9
Producer Hedging	15.2	19.0	1.3	26.7	-	9.2	-	69.1	5.5	-	
Implied Net Disinvestment	49.4	51.5	102.6	129.3	153.8	100.2	158.8	92.5	49.0	79.5	
Total Supply	724.2	725.2	739.8	780.7	775.3	777.4	823.9	857.5	836.0	888.2	7928.2

15

Demand											
Fabrication											
Industrial Applications	273.5	266.8	259.3	269.8	281.4	295.3	297.3	320.4	316.7	343.2	
Photography	221.1	216.2	210.3	210.1	213.1	220.5	224.6	233.0	244.6	246.4	
Jewelry & Silverware	188.7	194.5	211.8	259.3	227.9	236.9	263.9	274.9	248.7	260.8	2367.4
Coins & Medals	34.0	31.3	33.5	41.5	43.8	24.7	23.3	28.5	26.1	27.0	313.7
Total Fabrication	717.4	708.9	714.9	780.7	766.2	777.4	809.1	856.8	836.0	877.4	
Net Official Sector Purchases	6.8	16.3	24.9	-	-	-		0.7	-	-	
Producer Hedging	,	-		-	9.1	-	14.8	-	-	10.8	
Total Demand	724.2	725.2	739.8	780.7	775.3	777.4	823.9	857.5	836.0	888.2	

So now let's look at the totals for this time period. It shows about 1.6 billion ounces coming from scrap and about 2.6 billion ounces that went into jewelry, silverware and coins. Even if no silver came from recovery from industrial processes and film, there is still a net increase in above-ground supplies of at least a billion ounces.

So here is my next to last table:

World Silver – Supply and Demand 2000 – 2009

Year	2000	2001	2002	2003	2004	2005	2006	2007	2008	2009	
Supply											
Mine Production	591.0	606.2	593.9	596.6	613.0	636.8	640.9	664.4	684.7	709.6	
Net Government Sales	60.3	63.0	59.2	88.7	61.9	65.9	78.2	42.5	27.6	13.7	
Old Silver Scrap	180.7	182.7	187.5	183.9	183.7	186.0	188.0	181.8	176.0	165.7	1816.0
Producer Hedging		18.9			9.6	27.6		-			
Implied Net Disinvestment	87.1		12.6				-				
Total Supply	**919.1**	**870.9**	**853.1**	**869.3**	**868.2**	**916.3**	**907.2**	**888.7**	**888.3**	**889.0**	
Demand											

Fabrication											
Industrial Applications	374.2	335.6	340.1	350.8	367.6	407.0	427.0	456.1	443.4	352.2	
Photography	218.3	213.1	204.3	192.9	178.8	160.3	142.4	124.8	104.9	82.9	
Jewelry	170.6	174.3	168.9	179.2	174.8	173.8	166.3	163.5	158.3	156.6	1686.3
Silverware	96.4	106.1	83.5	83.9	67.2	67.5	61.0	58.4	56.9	59.5	740.4
Coins & Medals	32.1	30.5	31.6	35.7	42.4	40.0	39.8	39.7	65.2	78.7	435.7
Total Fabrication	891.7	859.4	828.3	842.4	830.8	848.7	836.4	842.5	828.6	729.8	
Producer De-Hedging	27.4		24.8	20.9			6.8	24.2	11.6	22.3	
Implied Net Investment		11.4		6.0	37.4	67.6	64.0	22.0	48.2	136.9	
Total Demand	**919.1**	**870.9**	**853.1**	**869.3**	**868.2**	**916.3**	**907.2**	**888.7**	**888.3**	**889.0**	

Once again, these numbers are in millions of ounces, with totals to the right. Add them up. You will see that for this 10-year period, above-ground supplies of silver increased by at least another billion ounces.

Part 2 – Picking Apart the Pundits

I just read what I think are a couple of *very* well-written analyses of silver production and demand since 3000 BC – with a few very big and important exceptions. The author of both is David Zurbuchen.

I don't mean to pick on this particular author. In fact, I congratulate him on the thoroughness of his numbers and the fact that he actually tries to provide some basis for his bullish position. However, plenty of silver "bulls" make the same errors of omission.

Perhaps this is a good time to repeat what I said on page six about demand. The bullish position is based largely upon the price ratio of silver to gold, compared with the production ratio of silver to gold. This ignores the relative demand for silver, which is at least as important – if not more so – than the amount produced.

In the first paper, "*The World's Cumulative Gold and Silver Production*" (http://www.gold-eagle.com/editorials_05/zurbuchen011506.html), the author gives several estimates of world production of gold and silver since 3000 BC. The average given for silver production is 44.542 billion ounces. Keep this number in mind.

The ratio of silver to gold production since 3000 BC is about 10.5 to 1. The author therefore concludes that the price of gold SHOULD be 10.5 times the price of silver.

Since the actual sales price of gold is more on the order of 50 times the price of silver – and has recently risen to as much as 70 times more than silver – the bullish rationale is that silver is due to go up dramatically. (Of course, one could use the same logic to argue that gold is about to *drop* dramatically).

Again, this reasoning ignores the actual demand for each commodity. The lack of supply – or abundance of supply – of anything is only *part* of the picture. It may or may not affect the demand for it.

For example, consider oil. Far more oil has been produced and exists than silver. Yet today, the price of a barrel of oil is about 3 times that of silver. Can I use this logic to conclude that silver is likely to go up dramatically in price? Or that the price of oil is likely to go down? No. We all know that the price of oil is dictated as much (or more so) by the huge demand for it than by the existing supply.

The price of anything – and everything – depends upon *both* its supply and the demand for it. This basic economic fact of life is often ignored by the silver bulls.

The "Missing" Silver

In the second paper, "*The Silver Deficit (1942-2004)*," (http://www.gold-eagle.com/editorials_05/zurbuchen040906.html) Mr. Zurbuchen argues that, from 1942 to 2004, the world used more silver than it mined. He estimates the total world demand, since the year 1900, at 36.9466 billion ounces of silver. Based upon his figures, he concluded that the world has consumed 6.2322 billion more ounces of silver than it has produced during that period.

As a starting point, let's assume that the numbers given by Mr. Zurbuchen are correct. 44.542 billion ounces produced since 3000 BC minus

36.9466 ounces used would leave 7.5954 billion ounces remaining in above-ground stocks (in the form of coins, jewelry, bars, silverware, etc). This assumes, with good justification, that silver used prior to 1900 was still in circulation as of 1900. There just weren't any uses of silver that would have logically led to it being "lost" to the world.

In addition, the demand numbers he uses assume that all silver that was used to meet the demand was somehow lost to the world. It ignores the fact that the silver used for coins, jewelry, silverware, and bars of silver is almost entirely still in circulation. Silver items are seldom thrown away! Just as an example, I am giving below a table I created showing production and silver amounts involved in some U.S. silver coins:

Total Silver Used in the Production of Various US Coins

Coin	Number Made	ASW	Silver Used
Morgan Dollar	657,000,000.00	0.77	508,150,080.00
Peace Dollar	190,577,000.00	0.77	147,399,874.88
Barber Half			0.00
Walking Liberty Half	485,395,040.00	0.36	175,683,880.78
Franklin Half	452,000,000.00	0.36	163,596,880.00
1964 Kennedy	433,000,000.00	0.36	156,720,020.00
Standing Liberty Quarter	226,792,000.00	0.18	41,042,548.24
Washington Quarter to 1964	3,795,988,590.00	0.18	686,960,055.13
Mercury Dime	2,673,932,528.00	0.07	193,560,627.84

Roosevelt Dime to 1964	6,566,055,420.00	0.07	475,303,619.74
Total Silver Used			2,548,417,586.61
Known Melted Dollars	270,000,000.00	0.77	208,828,800.00
Minimum Silver in Un-melted Coins Worldwide Prior to 1990			2,339,588,786.61

You'll note that I don't give the numbers for Barber Silver Halves. I also don't even have Trade Dollars, Barber Dimes, Barber Quarters, the silver war nickels made from 1942 to 1945, or the 40% Silver Kennedy's made from 1965 to 1970 in the table. I have also subtracted off the Silver Dollars that were known to have been melted by the US just after World War I. Note that the total is about 2.3 Billion ounces. Now I am not about to argue that all of this 2.3 Billion is still in circulation. I don't doubt that some of it has been melted down and used for other purposes. But we do know that a lot of it is still around. And I haven't put *all* silver coins made by the U.S. in this table. And I haven't started talking about the amount of silver in coins made by Britain, Germany, France, Spain, *etc*. During much of this period the British Empire dominated the world and it would only be reasonable that there were a lot more British coins around. And we know that although some have been melted there are still quite a few around. It isn't hard to conclude that there are *at least a couple Billion* ounces of silver in the form of coins dating prior to 1990 that are still with us.

Even More Silver

For much of history, there are no good figures regarding the amount of silver used in jewelry and silverware. However, if we look at the data given above for the period from 1990 to 2009, jewelry and silverware accounted for about 28 percent of the worldwide silver demand.

Let's apply the modern percentage to the demand of 36.9466 ounces since 1900. The result is 10.345 billion ounces. This would then mean there are another 10.345 billion ounces of silver around the world as an above-ground resource. Add this to the figure above and you get 17.94 billion ounces of silver in total above-ground resources (*not* including coins).

Also, consider this. While we do not know the amount of silver recovered from photography and electronics, we do know that silver *is* recovered from those sources. So, while it can be argued that there are factors that may reduce the figure of 17.94 billion ounces of silver from above-ground resources, there are also factors that would increase it. I believe there is good justification for thinking that the factors that would increase this number outweigh the factors that would reduce it.

Things to Consider

Nowhere in this book have I told you *not* to buy silver. Nowhere in this book do I tell you to buy silver. Much of the above ground resources that I mention above are in the form of coins, jewelry, and silverware. At what price do you sell your silver jewelry? Do you have a highly graded Morgan that has a book price of $1000? You wouldn't sell that if silver got to $100 per ounce, would you? The point is that while there may be a *lot* more silver in the world than many pundits would have you believe, the price at which it is made available to the market is also likely more than the current price, about $36 per ounce.

Conclusion

So … have you read that there is only about one billion ounces in above-ground silver in existence? Or that JP Morgan Chase was supposedly short 3.3 billion ounces, and that this amount was more silver than existed above-ground?

Let's forget the gaps in our knowledge and go with what we *do* know:

From 1990 to 2009, above-ground sources of silver ***increased*** by at least 2 billion ounces.

Quite a few silver coins made prior to 1990 are still around.

Much of the silver jewelry and silverware ever produced is still in existence.

Some silver used in electronics and photography is reclaimed.

Based upon the facts outlined here, I believe that stories claiming that there are only one billion above-ground ounces of silver in the world are, simply, hogwash. There also are plenty of reasons to believe there is a LOT more silver out there.

I believe that it would even be possible for an extremely wealthy bank to have as much as 3.3 billion ounces of silver *in its possession*. I also believe that if the banking interests wanted *you* to know this, *they* would have written this paper.

Contacting the author:

I live, work, and make best efforts to play in Missoula, Montana. I can best be reached via email at cssiwill@earthlink.net.

12200281R00019

Made in the USA
Lexington, KY
29 November 2011